W9-BGM-774

R

Restoring Relationships

The Importance of *Forgiving* and *Being Forgiven*

by

Ralph A. Gwinn

Restoring Relationships
Copyright © 2001 by Ralph A. Gwinn
ALL RIGHTS RESERVED

Fairmont Books
P.O. Box 3595
Hagerstown, MD   21742-3595
www.mcdougalpublishing.com

ISBN 1-58158-052-5

Printed in the United States of America
For Worldwide Distribution

DEDICATION

To my wife, MAUREEN, with thankfulness for the richness of our years together.

ACKNOWLEDGMENTS

I have a very great indebtedness to many people. One of the difficulties of writing in the later years of one's life is the problem of identifying the precise persons. Over the years, insights from many sources have become so much a part of my own thinking that they are no longer traceable, but the debt remains very large. Specific quotations from published sources are easy enough to identify, and I am grateful for the help those authors have provided.

David Augsburger is an example of both sides. His *Caring Enough to Forgive/Caring Enough to Not Forgive* is the specific book that triggered my own desire to do some study of forgiveness. My book is the end result of the process that began in the early 1980s. I quote Augsburger a number of times. Beyond that, anyone familiar with his work will recognize my indebtedness to him. I gladly acknowledge how much his study has meant to me. If my book can be as profitable to others as his book has been to me, I shall be abundantly rewarded.

One of my seminary professors, Edward J. Carnell, is another who has enriched my thinking tremendously. Specifically, his book *Christian Commitment* is profoundly powerful. Alas, it is no longer in print. He was especially helpful on the relationship between justice and forgiveness.

I would also like to make special mention of Melody Goddard Rhode. Melody, the daughter of longtime and very close friends, Homer and Isabelle Goddard, earned a Ph.D. in clinical psychology. Her dissertation, "Forgiveness, Power and Empathy," provided some challenging insights.

Over the years, my involvement with people in a variety of situations has enriched my life and provided insights into forgiveness. I thank all those unnamed people.

As I began the process of writing, I enlisted the help of a few family members and close friends. I sent them a number of pages at a time asking them to critique the material. That process proved to be immensely valuable to me and has greatly strengthened this study. My "elect" group was made up of my wife, Maureen (whose help and encouragement and love go far beyond comments on the text); our daughter, Cathy Thwing; a sister-in-law, Polly Gwinn; a brother, the Rev. William Gwinn; a longtime friend, the Rev. Richard Grout; a former colleague and close friend from Tarkio College, Dr. Larry Pattee; two staff colleagues from Rose Hill Presbyterian Church, the Rev. Brad Buff and

Mrs. Debbie Jacobson; a member of that church and a friend, Randy Foldvik. I must make particular mention of the help of Larry Pattee and Randy Foldvik. They often replied with letters of three, four or five pages. Their questions and suggestions were very valuable. My responses to them as well as the others often were incorporated into the text.

I wish also to thank the Rev. Earl Palmer, both my pastor and friend, for his perceptive comments on the text. I am especially indebted to him for writing the foreword.

I am grateful to Readable, Ink., and, in particular, to Janet Moneymaker, co-owner, for her illustrations and layout.

Mrs. Lois Curley provided valuable editorial comments.

Thanks to the staff of McDougal Publishing for their care and help.

CONTENTS

Foreword

Karl Barth described forgiveness as "the power of all powers." It is the grand and generous result in our lives of the grace of God. When I first heard a lecture by Dr. Ralph Gwinn on the meaning of forgiveness, I was deeply impressed by the wisdom and wholeness of the man who was the teacher. Here is a scholar and pastor who understands the forgiveness of Jesus Christ as "the power of all powers."

Ralph Gwinn has lived his own life in the daily journey of grace so that what he has written for us in this vital book on forgiveness is both exciting and relevant.

Those of us who have been colleagues of Dr. Gwinn have urged him to write this book, and now I am pleased that it is a reality. We need this book.

Earl F. Palmer
University Presbyterian Church
Seattle, Washington

INTRODUCTION

The story of redemption began with the fall of man in Genesis 3. God graciously and immediately started the process of renewal, which culminated in the life, death and resurrection of Jesus Christ. Today, we are living "between the times" of the first and second comings of Christ. When we respond to the provision of God in Christ, there is a new birth (see John 3:3-7), a new creation (see 2 Corinthians 5:17), the beginning of a lifelong growth. That growth takes place both in our understanding and in our behavior, as we undergo an ongoing development of our likeness to Christ. This process is the work of the Holy Spirit, and the goal is to enable us to *be holy* (Leviticus 19:2 and 1 Peter 1:16).

In this process of becoming like Christ, there is one essential element that is often overlooked. Because we never get to the place where we no longer sin against God and against one another, forgiveness is essential to maintaining forward motion in the process. In a very real sense, each of us is God's "great work," and He continues to work to make us better likenesses of Christ, both as individuals and together as the Body of Christ. But God's "problem" is that we aren't always as eager for that likeness as He is, and so we drag our feet. Some people even refuse to let Him *start* the process with them. This book is an attempt to help us understand what is involved in forgiveness, with a view to enriching our lives with God and with one another.

Ralph A. Gwinn
Seattle, Washington

Chapter 1

BEGINNING THE QUEST

Be kind and compassionate to one another,
forgiving each other, just as in Christ God
forgave you. Ephesians 4:32

MY EARLIEST RECOLLECTION of a forgiveness-related experience was being told to sit in a chair in a corner
until I was willing to say, "I'm sorry." I never recall
the other side, being told to sit in a corner until I
was willing to forgive a brother or sister (I was one
of eight children) who had hurt me. Authentic forgiveness requires both elements, a genuine spirit
of forgiveness on the part of the person wronged
and a genuine expression of sorrow on the part of
the offender. When both attitudes meet, forgiveness takes place.

Restoring Relationships

In my childhood, forgiveness was not often talked about. My family always went to church. In the process, I learned the Lord's Prayer (probably by osmosis), with its *"Forgive us our debts as we forgive our debtors."* I don't recall any specific teaching about what that clause in the prayer meant.

We children learned a prayer common in that era, always repeated at bedtime: *"Now I lay me down to sleep; I pray the Lord my soul to keep. If I should die before I wake, I pray the Lord my soul to take. Lord, bless ...,"* and family members were named. There was nothing about forgiveness in the prayer. Indeed, the prayer had a solitary focus: keep my soul either while I sleep or in the event of my death during the night. I don't remember ever hearing a comparable morning prayer for the day.

A forced repentance ("sit there until ...") may be a step above no repentance at all, but I quickly learned that the magic words "I'm sorry" freed me from that "prison." So the words often taught hypocrisy more than anything else. The "real sorrow" was to be caught! Although in my family I saw little parental practice of genuinely expressing "I'm sorry" or of showing a spirit of forgiveness, I don't believe our family was abnormal in that respect.

My own relationship with my father was a source of grief to me over many years. I relate it as an example that I will refer to from time to time by way of illustration.

I was the third boy in our family. My mother died less than two weeks after I was born. My father subsequently remarried, and there were five more children: three boys and two girls. As we children grew up, there never was any sense of "we" versus "them" from either side — at least that was my perception.

Early on, I became aware of the fact that my father was always "on my case." I don't mean that he was physically abusive. I simply could never do anything well enough to please him. For example, a school holiday was usually anticipated. For me, Washington's Birthday was not a happy occasion. I hated the day. We had a large garden, and every year Washington's Birthday marked the first planting of peas. Peas had to be planted in a particular pattern. If I planted them straight enough to please my father, I was not fast enough; if I was fast enough, the peas were not straight enough. I could not win. If I was a partner with my father in croquet, I was always told what shot to make (or attempt) when it was my turn. The fear of missing the shot did not encourage success! There is no need for multiple examples. My failure to please my father was not from my lack of trying! My sense of helplessness was heightened because I could never understand the reason I did not measure up to his expectations.

Near the end of my first year in college I learned of an opportunity for summer work with the Weyerhauser Lumber Company in the Northwest. The manager, a committed Christian, was recruiting Christian college men to work in the woods with the company's loggers.

Such a job would provide help with college expenses. More importantly to me, one of the manager's explicit goals was to have the summer employees work alongside the loggers and be ready to share Christ with them. The idea appealed to me very much, and I came to the conclusion that it was God's will for me to apply. I broached the idea to my father, assuming his ready assent. My assumption rested on the fact that spending the summer in that way involved two things high on his scale of values: hard work and money. To my surprise, he said a very emphatic no.

Over the ensuing days, our respective positions became more rigidly fixed. Because I believed it was God's will for me to try for it, I could see nothing else. I was nineteen, living at home, and my father was paying my college expenses. These were factors that did not enter the equation in my thinking.

One morning, as I was getting ready to leave for school, my father came to my room, closed the door, leaned against it and said to me, "You broke my heart once; I will not let you do it again. If you go ahead with this scheme, do not come back home." Then he turned and left the room. I was dumbfounded!

After further consideration, I decided to go ahead with the application. When I told the man who was handling the applications what had happened, he said that they would not accept my application under those conditions. That was how the matter was resolved. I reported that fact to my father, and neither of us ever spoke of it again. (Interestingly, many years later I was chatting with the man who had proposed the summer program. He told me the plan never materialized, for a variety of reasons. Still, the proposal had a profound effect on my life!)

My father's statement made clear the reason for the problem we had had through the years — he had blamed me for the death of my mother! To blame an infant for the death of his mother is altogether irrational as well as wrong, but it was nonetheless real. That part of what he said was clear enough immediately.

Another part of what he said didn't sink in for more than forty years. I heard his words, but I didn't hear what I now think the words involved. "I will not let you [break my heart] again" — is that not an expression of love? His heartbreak was something neither he nor I could have prevented. My father was not one to express his love in ways I understood as a child or a youth. I think it fair to say that my ongoing experience of endlessly feeling put down had deafened me to any oblique expression of his love. His heartbreak in the death of my mother was understandable. The ways he expressed that heartbreak toward me remained a mystery to me.

Dad was a good father in many ways. He provided well for his family — no mean accomplishment through the years of the Depression with eight children. We lived in a lovely home. Most of us had music lessons. Although my father never got as far as high school himself, each of us went to college, three of us receiving one or more graduate degrees. He paid a large part of the cost of undergraduate education for all of us. He also made sure that the six of us boys learned how to work. My father had a sense of humor, though it was sometimes expressed at the expense of others. We regularly attended church. We had many good experiences as a family.

I make no mention here of the only person I ever knew as a mother in these memories of my growing-up years. Although aware that the good things I enjoyed then could not have been mine apart from her, I have focused on my relationship with my father and the insights that relationship provided for my understanding of forgiveness. Laudable qualities do not remove the harm that one human being can do to another. Only a full-orbed forgiveness can do that. What that "full-orbed" forgiveness entails will become apparent as the book unfolds.

In my youth, I often heard that I could not do anything well, which I gradually interpreted to mean that I could scarcely do things even adequately. My failure to win approval from my father left me with little confidence in who I was and what I was capable of doing. That is a painful heritage. Reading became one avenue of escape. Also, though still immature in my Christian faith, I understood, at least dimly, that I had value in God's eyes.

God used two experiences in a single weekend to give me a new and growing sense of genuine self-worth. In the spring that I turned nineteen I attended a weekend Inter-Varsity Christian Fellowship conference. One of the speakers that particular weekend emphasized the truth that Christ lives in the Christian, e.g., Galatians 2.20: *"I stand crucified with Christ; it is no longer I who live but Christ lives in me ..."* (my rendering). This truth came through with special clarity in the Saturday evening session. For me, that truth was simply revolutionary: If Christ lives in me, then I am of genuine worth, of value — and no one can take the reality of Christ's presence from me! The wonder of that truth (and its sharp contrast with my earlier poor image of myself) has continued to warm my heart through the ensuing years.

The second experience that reinforced the turnaround of my attitude toward myself involved a young woman who attended that same conference. We had known who the other was as the result of a high school class together. In addition, one of my sisters was a good friend of her sister, one of my brothers had dated her sister a few times, and we were in the same youth group at our church. That weekend, she caught my attention in a new way. How does one explain that kind of mystery? At the conference I so lacked confidence in myself that I would only sit where I could see her.

I screwed up my courage and asked that young lady, for our first date, to a Seattle church during the following week. We went to hear the Inter-Varsity conference speaker who had been used of God to touch me very deeply the previous weekend. Just to ask her to go with me was a major step! Our relationship grew quickly into friendship, then love, and three and a half years later, Maureen and I were married.

I do not know what other people saw in me following that conference. I do have some clear ideas of what began to happen within me. And it was all powerfully positive!

Maureen's growing care about me simply because I was "me" relieved me of any required performance, conditions or demands. (I did not have to plant the peas straight enough and fast enough!) There were no demands. Being loved unconditionally by this one person freed me in relationships with other people. However others (my father, in particular) regarded me, I now had one secure, tangible relationship. The implications of that reality did not spring instantly into place, but the foundation was there upon which new relationships could be built.

The first time I sensed any pride in me on my father's part came when I finished my flight training, received my wings and was commissioned an officer in the Army Air Corps early in World War II. I was twenty-two.

How could a father blame an infant for the death of his mother? This question haunted me as I grappled with the relational problem between my father and me. Did I not have some responsibility for reaching out for a measure of reconciliation? Yes, I did, though I never made the slightest overture in that direction before my father died, more than thirty-five years ago. I think the reason was partly my deep-seated and long-standing fear of my father. Fear and love make strange bedfellows.

Still, why wasn't my newfound sense of who I am "in Christ" enough to move me toward healing the strained relationship with my father? Did I too gladly hold tight to my resentment? Was I being as "generous" in spirit toward my father as I was toward myself? Did I look for factors in his life that boxed him in to blaming me for my mother's death?

Regretfully, the answers to these questions for many years were the wrong ones. I was slow to accept any responsibility for my attitudes, and quick to blame him for his. My father could not say, quite simply, "I was wrong in saying [or doing] what I did. I am truly sorry that I hurt you." And I did not yet understand the meaning of a spirit of forgiveness.

Healthy solutions to problems of broken relationships are not usually worked out quickly or easily. My father and I both seemed unable to accept our individual responsibility for changing our own responses to the other.

Genuinely forgiving my father did not come easily for me. Although I became able to say the words to myself (long after his death), it was some time before the reality of forgiveness was there. After I believed I had truly forgiven him, I still found some dark, unwelcome pockets of continuing resentment. One year our daughter gave me as a birth-day gift Lewis Smedes' book *Forgive and Forget.* I began to see that I had hated my father for years. To use Smedes' distinction (in chapter 2), mine had not been an aggressive hatred, but rather a passive, smoldering hate deep within me. This insight shocked me.

Stemming from the hurts of the past, that hatred had been as destructive to me as to my father. Hatred of a person precludes the development of a healthy relationship with that person. Hatred also diminishes the hater's capacity to love. Although my father was dead, I was still unconsciously carrying seeds of hate. This realization sharply reminded me that I had much to learn about the healing of strained and broken relationships.

Forgiveness always presupposes a problem. The problem basically is a bent or fractured relationship. The number of stressful personal relationships is legion. One example of such a relational problem is the high rate of divorce in our country, with its frequent and tragic estrangement for children. A marriage normally begins with joy and the expectation of permanence in the relationship. In reality, disagreements, hurts, accusations enter and one or the other, often both, are wounded. Too often there is not adequate effort to heal the wounds.

Restoring Relationships

Additional hurts compound the problem. After a while, it seems easier to sever the relationship than to heal it.

Other kinds of problem relationships are found in business, education, friendships, sports, etc. There are many examples of bent or broken ties that need mending. "Left alone, cracks widen, and for the resulting chasms of ungrace there is only one remedy: the frail rope-bridge of forgiveness" (Yancey, *What's So Amazing About Grace?*, p. 84).

Learning the richness of forgiveness is often a slow process. Part of the reason is that forgiveness is not only cognitive. It goes beyond simply understanding what the barriers are to healthy relationships and how to remove them. The more fundamental problem is volitional. We are often unwilling to admit that we do not care enough to learn what was in the mind of the one who wronged us and to approach that person with a view to talking through what we see as the problem. Often enough, one person hurts another without realizing it.

The nature and process of forgiving in God's way is the focus of the chapters that follow. This introductory chapter already suggests some pressing questions: (1) How do the two elements of forgiveness, a spirit of forgiveness and repentance, become realities in our relationships? (2) What is the goal of forgiveness — why bother with forgiveness? (3) If I am wronged, isn't there some place for justice — how do forgiveness and justice relate to each other?

The backdrop for all that follows is Paul's demanding prescription: *"Be kind and compassionate to one another, forgiving each other, just as in Christ God forgave you"* (Ephesians 4:32, see also Colossians 3:13). In all matters of forgiveness, God is both our Model and the very fount of forgiveness.

Because we hurt one another so easily, each of us has ample opportunities to say from the heart, "I'm sorry," and to maintain a spirit of forgiveness toward those who wrong us. None of us is exempt from struggling with forgiveness. Realization of how fully God has forgiven us is clouded by our own demands that justice be met to our satisfaction before we consider forgiving another. We do not understand that in Christ the legitimate claims of justice are already met. (See Chapter 4 for a development of this truth.)

Forgiveness of those we believe have wronged us in significant matters rarely comes all at once. More often forgiving is a painful process. Our will is slow to respond in the way God asks. Our growth in the willing and doing of forgiveness is helped if we keep returning to the model God sets before us.

I close this introductory chapter with three

thoughtful and heartwarming statements regarding forgiveness:

- Lewis Smedes, in his book *Forgive and Forget*, calls forgiveness "love's antidote for hate" (p. 47).
- Henri Nouwen states, "Forgiveness is the name of love practiced among people who love poorly" ("Forgiveness: The Name of Love in a Wounded World," in *Weavings*, Vol. VII, Number 2, March/April 1992, p. 15).
- Melody Goddard Rhode, in an unpublished Ph.D. dissertation in clinical psychology, says, "For this investigation, forgiveness is defined simply as, a process of actively replacing injury with love" (*Forgiveness, Power, and Empathy*, p. 9).

Questions for Discussion

1. What is your earliest recollection of any experience or teaching regarding forgiveness?

2. What is your own present understanding of forgiveness? Do you have any feel as to how your present understanding of forgiveness came about?

3. In which of your relationships do you find the greatest struggle regarding forgiveness? Do you find that your closest relationships are the most difficult to work through to forgiveness? If so, why do you think that is the case?

Chapter 2

PREREQUISITES TO FORGIVENESS?

*"Shouldn't you have had mercy on your fel-
low servant just as I had on you?"*

Matthew 18:33

THERE *ARE* PREREQUISITES to forgiveness. What do I
mean by prerequisites? I do not speak of them in
the sense of some "hoops" we need to jump
through, nor a kind of obstacle course we need to
negotiate. I do not mean in any sense that the prerequisites are a means of earning forgiveness. They
are not mechanical, not arbitrary, not "if we do our
part, God will do His." Always, in the biblical por-
trayal, the initiative is God's. He is the one who has

provided the basis for our salvation in Christ's death and resurrection.

John 3:16 states the matter simply and directly: *"For God so loved the world that he gave his one and only Son, that whoever believes in him shall not perish but have eternal life."* The prerequisites I speak of are simply means of making clear our response to God's prior action. The two prerequisites I name are simply terms for what is essential in a good relationship, whether with God or with people. It is not at all necessary that the terms be used. What is essential is that the attitudes the terms represent be present.

Any kind of relationship has at least two parties. When the closeness of the relationship is broken, healing requires a particular attitude on each side.

For the person wronged there must be an openness to the wrongdoer, a real desire for the closeness to be restored. I am calling that attitude in the wronged person "a spirit of forgiveness." For the wrongdoer, the appropriate attitude is called "repentance," a genuine expression of sorrow for having hurt the other person.

A Spirit of Forgiveness

The first element necessary for forgiveness is the attitude of the wronged person, namely a "spirit of forgiveness." At the human level, if I am wronged by another person, I have a responsibility to be open to the person, to care for the person. I must leave aside resentment and bitterness. I must want God's best for the person. I must seek reconciliation. In a word, I must deal with the other as God deals with me (see Ephesians 4:32), not an easy thing to do!

We are not like calculators where the previous problem is cleared and we start anew. While recognizing the reality that pain takes time to dissipate, there are two important cautions. One is that we do not fall into the trap of self-pity because of the wrong we experienced. It is very easy to nurse the pain and pat ourselves on the back that we "forgave" the other. That attitude is destructive to a relationship.

The other caution is that we too easily gloss over our fault. For instance, where there is unfaithfulness in a marriage by either partner, the overt unfaithfulness of the "guilty" one gets the attention. What about the deep pain the "innocent" party may have caused the other by the absence of expression of love, by neglect, by thoughtlessness, etc. Very often the sharp hurt to one person in a relationship has its counterpart in the hurt experienced by the other. The important point is that forgiveness is not accomplished by one person.

Restoring Relationships

When we have experienced God's level of forgiveness, how can we, how dare we, refuse to manifest a spirit of forgiveness toward one who has wronged us? Jesus emphasized this reality very sharply in his story in Matthew 18:21-35. Peter came to Him with a question, *"How often must I forgive one who has wronged me, as many as seven times?"* (my rendering). I suspect Peter thought he was being very generous in suggesting seven times. As a matter of fact, he was. We do not often forgive a person who wrongs us significantly and in the same way as many as seven times.

Two of my brothers were partners in a construction business a few years ago. On one occasion when they needed a new accountant, one of their pastors encouraged them to hire a qualified person who was just being released from prison after serving a sentence for embezzlement. With some hesitation, they agreed to do so. Things went fine for a time. Then one weekend the accountant absconded with sixty thousand dollars of their money. It would be difficult to get them to hire another person under the same circumstances once more. Would they do so seven times?

Jesus told a startled Peter that seven times was hardly a start, there is no limit to the number of times we need to forgive another. He underscored that truth by a story. A king wanted to settle

36

Prerequisites to Forgiveness?

accounts with his servants. They were called in one by one. One servant owed his master an astronomical figure, ten thousand talents. The New Revised Standard Version has a footnote which says that one talent would be equal to more than fifteen years' wages of a laborer. At that rate, it would take more than a hundred and fifty thousand years to earn ten thousand talents! Since the servant could not pay, the king ordered him, his family and anything he had to be sold to apply against the debt. The servant pleaded for time (he did not ask for forgiveness of the debt) and said he would repay the debt. The master had compassion on him and even canceled that huge debt.

The same servant, as he went out from that experience, met a fellowservant who owed him a hundred denarii. At a denarius per day (the usual pay for a worker), that would be the wages for three and a third months. The forgiven man seized him by the throat and demanded payment. That debtor also pleaded for time, but he was refused and was thrown into prison.

The other servants reported the matter to the king. He was furious and called in the man whose debt had been canceled. "How is this possible?" he asked in effect. "I forgave you that enormous debt. Should you not have had mercy on your colleague who owed you a pittance by comparison, three and a third months' wages versus a hundred and fifty thousand years' wages?" And the king had him thrown into prison. Then Jesus uttered the awesome punch line: *"This is how my heavenly Father will treat each of you unless you forgive your fellow human being from your heart"* (my rendering). A failure to manifest the spirit of forgiveness is itself a very great wrong.

Had Jesus left the last three words off, the story would not have had the same force. We could have said, "Oh, yes, I forgave the person," without giving much attention to what forgiveness means. But the words "from your heart" involve a genuineness we cannot easily escape. "It may be an infinitely less evil to murder a man than to refuse to forgive him. The former may be the act of a moment of passion; the latter is the heart's choice" (George MacDonald, *An Anthology*, edited by C.S. Lewis, p. 6).

That last sentence of Jesus' parable catches us unexpectedly. Compare what Jesus says in Matthew 6:15: *"But if you do not forgive others their sins, your Father will not forgive you your sins"* (my rendering). The whole incident is saying in different words what Paul said in Ephesians 4:32. Our forgiveness of others must follow the pattern of God's forgiveness of us. He always has a spirit of forgiveness, and when God forgives us, it is "from the heart."

Prerequisites to Forgiveness?

How does a spirit of forgiveness arise? My spirit of forgiveness grows out of experiencing God's forgiveness. If I as a Christian have experienced the greatness of His forgiveness, I cannot defend any unwillingness to forgive one who has wronged me — however severe the wrong may be. As I grow in my appreciation of what God has done for me in Christ, I become more open and caring for others. In a word, I become more Christ-like. This process entails spending time in the Scriptures and in prayer, that is, in a growing relationship with God, and in fellowship with other Christians.

God's love for me moves me to love others. *"The commandment we have from [God] is this: those who love God must love their brothers and sisters also"* (1 John 4.21, NRS). Genuine love for others embodies a spirit of forgiveness. As love grows, a spirit of forgiveness grows.

One friend of mine raised this problem: "If God is our standard, what chance do I have?" My friend called such statements in Scripture as *"from your heart"* here or *"forgive us our debts as we forgive our debtors"* in Matthew 6:12 (my rendering), "scary." Regarding the latter quotation, Yancey writes: "What makes the 'as' so terrifying? The fact that Jesus plainly links our forgiven-ness by the Father with our forgiving-ness of fellow human beings" (*What's So Amazing About Grace?* p. 87). But are

Restoring Relationships

Jesus' statements set before us in a threatening fashion? No. God is not content with casual forgiveness and doesn't want us to be either. We must always be in a growing mode — relationships, understanding, attitudes, spirit of forgiveness, etc. To have a pattern is helpful, especially if the model is a good one. God says, "Follow My pattern."

While we can never follow God's pattern perfectly, we can keep improving, growing, maturing. C.S. Lewis makes a keen distinction between "pleased" and "satisfied" that is encouraging (*Mere Christianity*, Book IV, Chapter 9). God is never (fully) satisfied with where we are in this life, but He is pleased at every evidence of growth. When a baby begins to walk, the parents are not satisfied with a step or two and a fall, but they are as pleased as can be at the evidence of growth. It is so with God. In that sense, there need be no fearfulness. God wants us to grow to maturity. If five years after a child begins to walk, he or she still takes a step or two and falls, there is no joy on the part of the parents. God, too, is not pleased unless we keep growing and developing.

Another friend asked me, "Doesn't that kind of forgiveness mean that you will be taken advantage of, that you will become a 'doormat,' that people will 'walk all over you'?" If we approach forgiveness from a position of scorekeeping of hurts done to us, the "doormat" danger becomes relevant. If we approach forgiveness from a relational standpoint or, to put it even more strongly, from a love standpoint, then it is more difficult to misuse Jesus' statements. Genuine forgiveness is always tied to love, to caring for a person, to relationship. How else could Jesus have answered Peter in Matthew 18:22?

Forgiveness is not easy, but the standard remains God's own. Is God a "doormat" because He chooses to forgive endlessly in response to our repentance? That we sometimes may be taken advantage of is probably true. Does that fact change our responsibility? Not at all. It simply makes the offending person still more offensive and harder to forgive!

Our common excuse that we can't forgive some wrongs, that they are just too great, is not really valid. The wrongs that we experience from others are, in comparison with our wrongs against God, always of the "three and a third months" variety. I do not mean the wrongs don't hurt. The pain I experienced because my father blamed me for my mother's death was very deep. I am trying to underscore the magnitude of our wrongs against an absolutely holy and just God.

When we consider the really severe hurts we sometimes receive, looking at them by themselves makes them stand out in all their starkness and pain. When we see them against the backdrop of how we hurt God, then we perceive them as the "three and a third months" type. We have great trouble even beginning to understand what sin means to infinite holiness. "When the Holy One of God has been crucified as a blasphemer by the pious leaders of a pious people, the fact is blazoned forth that our holiness is still a blasphemy of God" (Koeberle, *The Quest for Holiness*, p. 57).

We get a glimpse of what sin means to infinite holiness at the cross, in the agonizing cry of our Lord, *"My God, my God, why have you forsaken me?"* (Matthew 27:46). For the absolute love and holiness of Christ to take on our sin — now we are talking about the "hundred and fifty thousand years" variety! The real truth is not that we can't, but that we won't — we refuse, we choose not to — express a spirit of forgiveness. The implication of this is troubling: God can forgive the person who wronged us; are we saying that our standards are higher than God's, that the repentance that leads to God's forgiveness is not sufficient to lead to our forgiveness? That is not a good position to be in!

Repentance

Repentance is a frequently used biblical word. The Hebrew word for repentance in the Old Testament is *shub*. It means "to turn around or return," not to turn around in the sense of spinning, but to turn around in terms of the direction one is going. The Greek term in the New Testament is *metanoia*, which means "a change of mind." In the biblical sense, we human beings are naturally self-centered. Sometimes that is reflected in our doing "bad" things; other times we may be doing useful, helpful things, or even nothing at all, but the center is wrong. Repentance means becoming God-centered. We do many of the same things (the useful types of things) as before, but now there is a new center.

Repentance involves a real change. If a person truly repents, God will receive him or her. There is a Rabbinic saying: "To enter upon a course of repentance and not to leave off sinning is compared to the man who enters a bath with the purpose of cleansing himself of a Levitical impurity, but keeps in his hands the dead reptile which is the cause of all this impurity" (Schechter, *Some Aspects of Rabbinic Theology*, pp. 334-335). All too often we keep carrying "the dead reptile"!

Is repentance portrayed in the Bible as one of the "hoops" one must go through to receive forgiveness? Emphatically not! It is simply impossible to maintain a friendship with another person if I am continually offending the person without expressing genuine sorrow for doing so. It is equally impossible to maintain a healthy relationship with God if I am continually offending Him and express no sorrow, "and a man who admits no guilt can accept no forgiveness" (C.S. Lewis, *The Problem of Pain,* p. 110).

Repentance is not something we generate in ourselves. Repentance is a response to the holiness of God. Isaiah's experience (see Isaiah 6) is a powerful example. He saw the glory of God and responded, *"Woe is me."* Now in the Christian era, in the shattering experience of catching something of the significance of Christ's death [*"God made him ... sin for us"* (2 Corinthians 5:21)], we cry out like the tax collector in Jesus' parable, *"God be merciful to me a sinner"* (Luke 18:13, KJV). We do not generate repentance; we simply can do nothing else against the backdrop of God's holiness. It is part of the work of the Holy Spirit to make us aware of our unholiness and thus quicken a sense of repentance. Palmer expresses it well: God doesn't compel us to repent but calls us to repent (*Revelation* in "The Communicator's Commentary," p. 155).

God has made forgiveness possible by the death and resurrection of His Son. He wants to forgive us, but He does not do so (at least usually) without our repentance. That is to say, because of His essential characteristic of holiness, it is simply not possible for Him to say, in effect, "Now, run along and be good children." To walk in our own self-centered way precludes walking in close fellowship with God or with another human being. We must choose to respond to God's provision. That choice is expressed in our repentance. Because *"God so loved the world that he gave his one and only Son"* (John 3:16) to solve the problem between us and Himself, and because His attitude as the wronged party is right (He has the spirit of forgiveness), doesn't mean that we are forgiven. It does mean that He has made forgiveness possible. For forgiveness to take place, that attitude or action of His must be met by our repentance, in other words, by some appropriate expression of sorrow. When we do this, we are forgiven!

Repentance is usually thought of with reference to the more obvious wrongdoer in the particular situation. We must also recognize, however, that a bent or broken relationship rarely involves fault on one side alone. One person is not often one hundred percent at fault and the other zero percent. It is fruitless to enter into some kind of attempt to ascertain how the blame should be divided, whether ninety-ten, sixty-forty or whatever. What is necessary is for the "wronged" person to acknowledge freely whatever part he or she also contributed to the problem.

Restoring Relationships

That does not mean saying, "If I hurt you, I'm sorry." Such a "repentance" comes across to the other as, "I wasn't at fault in any way, but if you think I was ..." That hardly qualifies as freely acknowledging my fault. Rather, I must say sincerely something like, "I, too, was at fault when I ..." or "I also offended you by ..." As Augsburger says, "People don't have problems alone and people do not find healing and forgiveness alone" (*Caring Enough to Forgive/Caring Enough to Not Forgive*, p. 26).

Augsburger emphasizes the necessity of repentance. At the end of each chapter he has three short segments that provide further material for meditation and study. At the end of chapter 4 of the *Caring Enough to Forgive* side of his book, he proposes discussion on "how sincere repentance is the only proper request for forgiveness" (p. 77). He then adds in parentheses a few very challenging lines:

> *I will not ask another for forgiveness. There are no biblical models for such in the New Testament. My part is confession and affirmation of repentance. If the other perceives this is genuine, forgiveness is given and received as a gift. If I ask for it, it is experienced as blackmail since to refuse, postpone, or to say "I'm not ready yet," is to appear to be "unforgiving."*

Prerequisites to Forgiveness?

Augsburger is not saying we should not ask God for forgiveness; he is speaking of not asking another human being.

Often we hurt another in a context of anger and are too proud to repent. Or we blame the other for the problem — "He [or she] is the one who should repent!" Or we hurt another accidentally and assume, since it was not deliberate, no repentance is necessary. The other will simply forgive me knowing that the hurt was accidental. We don't ask ourselves how the other would know that the hurt was accidental! Or we hurt another without knowing it and unless the other person makes the hurt known to us (and we humans are usually reluctant to do so), repentance is not a relevant concept.

A caution is worth mentioning. We see sins on a scale from minor sins (not too hurtful) to major sins (very damaging). The damage is not necessarily only to our psyche. Infidelity in marriage, for instance, can result in serious physical problems (such as herpes or AIDS) in addition to the emotional devastation. We determine the level of hurt in a subjective manner. Hence our various lists are quite different. The difference is primarily in how the particular affront impacts us. For instance, in the abstract, I might not rate adultery as heinous a sin as another person would, but if my spouse was unfaithful to me, then my "rating" of the evil of the act would jump up sharply. On the basis of what we have in the Bible, we must recognize that no sin, however slight it may seem to us, can escape God's judgment, whether at the cross of Christ or ultimately upon the individual sinner directly.

Let me pause at this point to make an important distinction. There are two senses in which repentance is necessary for God's forgiveness. The first focuses on our initial turning to God.

We find ourselves becoming uneasy deep within ourselves. It may manifest itself in any number of ways. Perhaps it's a failure to live up to our own standards; perhaps we begin to see ourselves in relation to God, and the huge gap between where we are and His standard overwhelms us; perhaps it develops from the death of a person significant to us, and thinking about death arouses some sense of fear or deep loneliness; perhaps it is a feeling that one's life seems to be useless — powerfully pictured in the Old Testament book of Ecclesiastes; perhaps it is simply a vague feeling of restlessness. Augustine's often-quoted words are pertinent: "Thou hast made us for thyself and restless is our heart until it comes to rest in thee" (*Confessions,* Book I, chapter 1).

On one occasion a young man, both wealthy and good, came to Jesus. In the course of their conversation the young man expressed the emptiness that

many feel, *"What do I still lack?"* (Matthew 19:20).
The problem, as this young man perceived it, was
not wrongdoing. He was, in fact, a good man in
terms of our usual standards. The problem was with
the center, with the central reality of his being. The
motivating center of our lives, whatever the quality of our actions may be, is normally our own
desire; it is independence from God rather than dependence on and fellowship with God.

James expresses the problem of our own desire
very effectively when he says, *"Each one is tempted
when he is drawn away and lured by his own desire"*
(James 1:14, my rendering). Several translations (for
example, the NIV) use the phrase *"by his own evil
desire."* That is really not justified, and it twists the
important point James is making. The Greek word
is *epithumia*, a neutral word morally, though a
strong word. It is like our word *desire* in the sense
that a desire may be good or bad. The word itself
does not indicate any moral quality.

Paul uses the same word in Philippians 1:23,
where he says his desire is to depart and be with
Christ, obviously a good desire. It is, of course, true
that the context may sometimes make clear
whether the desire is good or bad, but I don't think
the context does that in James. Indeed, to use the
phrase "evil desire" suggests that temptation car-
ries with it the movement to do evil. That is not

always true, at least in the moral sense. We can be tempted to do something that is good in itself, which moves us from doing what is best in the context.

For example, it may be a good deed to give someone in need twenty-five dollars. It is still better to do something to help the person with his need for a job or for medical help for example. The desire to give twenty-five dollars is good, but it may keep us from doing that which is more necessary. The real problem that James points to is in the adjective *idios*, which means "one's own." The essential point is not that it is a desire, but that it is one's own desire without reference to God's desire. Whatever the content of the desire may be, if it is independent of any God-reference, the temptation is pulling us in the wrong direction. In the context of this study, an overemphasis on our "own desire" is destructive to good relationships.

The strength of the uneasiness and/or emptiness which brought the young man to Jesus, and which we often feel, may be the catalyst that moves a person to respond to Christ's invitation, *"Come to me, all you who are weary and burdened, and I will give you rest"* (Matthew 11:28). To come to Christ is the essential heart of repentance. The change that repentance calls for doesn't necessarily mean changing jobs or moving to a different place. It does

Prerequisites to Forgiveness?

mean a different center to one's life, a different core, a move from self-centeredness to God-centeredness, from my desire to God's desire. When we repent in that way, we experience God's forgiveness. All of the past failure, emptiness, wrongheadedness and wrongdoing stands forgiven.

What forgiveness essentially involves at this point is that the penalty for both the wrongbeing, the central problem, and the wrongdoing which flows from the wrongbeing is set aside, not ignored. God's holiness cannot permit that. If we accept Christ's identification with our sinfulness on the cross, everything is turned around for us — as Paul put it in 2 Corinthians 5:17, *"If anyone is in Christ, a new creation; the old went, the new has come"* (my rendering).

To accept God's provision is repentance. We come to Christ, and the penalty for all of our sins is wiped out because of Christ's death and resurrection. So Paul cries out, *"Therefore, there is now no condemnation for those who are in Christ Jesus"* (Romans 8:1). The new direction in our lives may be slower to become apparent! *"For you were called to freedom, brothers and sisters; only do not use your freedom as an opportunity for self-indulgence, but through love become slaves to one another"* (Galatians 5:13, NRS). "To become slaves to one another" does not happen overnight. It is an on-going process.

The second sense in which repentance is necessary for God's forgiveness has a parallel in the ordinary aspects of life. In any close human relationship (marriage, parent-child, friends, associates, etc.), we inevitably hurt one another. That spoils the closeness of the fellowship until repentance takes place and is met by a spirit of forgiveness, resulting in forgiveness. The same thing happens in our relationship with God. We offend God, and that spoils the closeness of our fellowship with Him — until we repent and experience His forgiveness. So repentance and forgiveness in this sense is an ongoing experience, something that happens over and over again. We are often rebellious or short-tempered or spiteful or impatient or whatever, but as often as we repent, that often He forgives. He always has the spirit of forgiveness. He does what He asks us to do with others, namely, to forgive without limit (see Luke 17:3-4). So in this sense, repentance and a spirit of forgiveness are a continuing need. As often as we offend God or a fellow human being, we need to express our repentance.

Repentance, then, is a concept that involves honest acknowledgment of our failure to honor God or people. Genuine repentance always involves the resolve that the wrongdoing will not be repeated. That is, there is a concrete turning from the old way. We don't always live up to the resolution, but the resolution is really there. One can hardly speak of repentance if that resolve is missing. Whenever I fail, repentance with its resolve to change is again called for.

One can also speak of repentance quite apart from any Christian understanding. Whenever we recognize that we have hurt another person, we acknowledge our fault, that is, we repent. Ordinary courtesy and justice require us to do so, though often enough we do not. If the other person meets our repentance with a spirit of forgiveness, the relationship is healed; in other words, forgiveness takes place.

When a relationship has been broken, there must be, to use Carnell's words, "a cordial spiritual willingness to accept the consequences of transgression" (*Christian Commitment*, p. 168). Or again, "Repentance cheerfully recognizes that it deserves condemnation, not forgiveness. It only inquires whether the offended party can forgive the very one who, on his own spiritual admission, is altogether unworthy of forgiveness" (p. 169). Or once again, "Whether in God or man, a person is powerless to extend forgiveness until the offending party meets the right moral conditions" (p. 254).

53

Restoring Relationships

But there must be not only a willingness but a desire for renewal on the part of the wronged person as well.

Philip Yancey has some hesitation regarding repentance as a requirement for forgiveness. He cites (*What's So Amazing About Grace?* pp. 103-104) the examples of the forgiveness of Jean Valjean by the bishop in Victor Hugo's great novel *Les Misérables,* where no repentance is evident in Valjean, and the forgiveness by Reginald Denny, a truck driver, of the two men who assaulted him during the turbulence in Los Angeles a few years ago. Again, there was no evidence of repentance on the part of the two men.

I find the resolution of this problem in using three terms instead of two. If we use *forgiveness* to represent both a spirit of forgiveness and the full restoration of the relationship, we often have confusion. If *forgiveness* is used for the outcome of repentance and a spirit of forgiveness, we can avoid the problem Yancey expresses so well. The bishop and Reginald Denny both expressed a spirit of forgiveness without regard to what the other did. Repentance would be necessary for the full restoration of fellowship.

Forgiveness does not undo the past. The actions, the hurts of the past cannot be changed — they really happened. We need to mitigate them to

Prerequisites to Forgiveness?

whatever extent is possible. One of the two thieves crucified with Jesus cried out to Him, *"Jesus, remember me when you come into your kingdom."* Jesus answered him, *"I tell you the truth, today you will be with me in paradise"* (Luke 23:42-43). The forgiveness the thief experienced then did not undo all of his crimes — they had actually happened, and his victims really suffered. His "death bed" conversion did not rewrite his history. It did change his relationship with God.

A common, but inadequate, expression is, "We simply have to forgive and forget." The expression's strength is that we are not to carry resentment and bitterness. However, the things that have happened to us are a part of our history. The weighty experiences of life we do not forget. Genuine forgiveness does enable us (most often gradually) to remember them without the searing hurt we experienced at the time the wrong took place, and to remember them without a deep feeling of resentment and bitterness. The sadness of the event may remain for a long time or even, in some cases, for the rest of one's life. If resentment and bitterness do not accompany that sadness, there is no critical problem. The physical damages that occurred may be permanent. For example, repentance does not restore the life of a child killed by a driver "under the influence" while the child was waiting for a school bus.

Restoring Relationships

To say that forgiveness should lead to forgetting the experience is too strong. Forgiveness does lead to a softening of the memory of the wrong. If the hurt was not too severe, the experience may slip out of our conscious memory over a period of time. In Christian forgiveness, the softening is enhanced by the Holy Spirit's working within us to bring healing and wholeness of spirit.

It is also true that forgiveness may transform the results of sin into positive blessings. Sometimes the positive side is simply: "I know how bad that hurt made me feel. I'll endeavor not to do that sort of thing to another." Sometimes the positive blessing is new growth in my own person so that I'm a better example of a growing Christian. Sometimes the blessing may be the end of a relationship that was really inimical to me as a person.

There are times when we extend a "grudging forgiveness." To put those two words together has a raspy sound and feel! Like a baby beginning to walk, such forgiveness is wobbly, but at least it is a start. Even if the forgiveness is not grudging, often it is only partial at the outset, due to our lack of understanding of ourselves. Not infrequently forgiveness is a process, sometimes a lengthy process, especially when there has been deep hurt. The new insight I had regarding my relationship with my father when I read Smedes' *Forgive and Forget* is

Prerequisites to Forgiveness?

an example (see p. 27); it is also a reminder that the process of forgiveness sometimes takes some years.

In this world, we humans must work with one another, interact with one another in a host of situations. We cannot have close fellowship if perceived wrong is present in the relationship. We often settle for whatever degree of closeness may be possible in the situation, but the "bentness" of the relationship keeps intruding to mar the wholeness that would otherwise be possible.

As I mentioned earlier, repentance on the offender's part involves implicitly, if not explicitly, the resolve not to offend again. Human experience in general, our own experience (each of us) in particular, clearly demonstrates that we fail in our resolution all too often! In other words, the risk of being hurt again is very high. Why should we run it? There are two good reasons.

The first is simply the incomparable beauty, wonder, joy, richness of a growing relationship between two persons. Sometimes the nature of the relationship does not hold much promise for that quality of closeness — for example, an alcoholic husband or wife in a marriage relationship, or an abusive parent with a young child. Such relationships are certainly destructive of trust. It seems like very hollow encouragement to say that some of these do get turned around, so hang on!

Restoring Relationships

That happens to be true, but it is just as true that many such situations do not get healed. So there is also the necessity for the realism to recognize that some human relationships are truly barren of any reasonable hope. We do live in a world that is far short of the beauty of Heaven! Of course we do not know in advance whether the relationship will be healed or not. Still, if a broken relationship can be healed, the result is eminently fine and satisfying. We need to do as much as we can in the given situation to bring about wholeness. We also need to recognize that miracles do sometimes happen in relationships.

The second reason for running the risk of being hurt repeatedly is our Model. How often does God run that risk with us? If the pattern for all of the factors involved in forgiveness is what God does, we must work at doing better than we commonly do in risking further hurt. Even though we cannot reach the level of God's "risking," we can let Him help us improve our problem relationships. God values our friendship, the closeness of our relationship with Him.

In Christ's great prayer in John 17, He prays at one point, *"Father, I want those you have given me to be with me where I am, and to see my glory"* (verse 24). What a marvelous expression of our Lord's desire for closeness with us! It is incredible that a growing closeness with Him does not move us more powerfully to a life walked in fellowship with His people as well. And who knows how far a wholesome example in our lives might go in helping another?

We must recognize that a static life is simply not what God wants. Indeed, are not the words *static* and *life* mutually contradictory? How can life be static? The very concept of life involves some degree of growth and change.

Does the value of the richness of a whole relationship need to be argued? Not really. It is common enough human experience that when a spirit of forgiveness and repentance bring healing to a problem relationship, the sense of joy and freedom and goodwill that follows on both sides is overwhelmingly satisfying and refreshing. That sense of "at-one-ness" becomes its own best argument.

Questions for Discussion

1. Do you find the categories of "spirit of forgiveness" and "repentance" convincing? Do they help to clarify some of the problems of forgiveness?

2. Have you had a particularly troubling relationship in which the "spirit of forgiveness" and "repentance" (had you been aware of them) might have helped to bring healing to the relationship? Are you willing to share your feelings in going through that experience?

3. As you think about problem relationships you have experienced, which seems more difficult to you, the "spirit of forgiveness" or "repentance"? Can you think of any reasons for your answer?

Chapter 3

THE GOAL OF FORGIVENESS

*"I have given them the glory that you gave
me, that they may be one as we are one."*
John 17:22

WHY FORGIVE? The goal of forgiveness lies in one
word, *community*. That word means "a unified
body of persons." The community may be a small
or a large unified body. Often in large communities there are subcommunities that may be very
much at odds with one another. For instance, the
community of the Church of Jesus Christ across the
world is divided into several smaller communities,
denominations, which are sometimes even antago-
nistic to each other. Or, in the political sense, the
former community of the U.S.S.R. is now divided

into many smaller states, some of which are very hostile to one another.

The idea of community as a unified body of persons is sharpened by noting the derivation of the word. Our English word comes from a pair of Latin words meaning "to belong to or to be shared by each of two parties." [Classical scholar Dr. Winifred Weter pointed out this derivation in conversation with the author.] Hence the goal of forgiveness is to restore a shared oneness by working through whatever problem or problems spoiled the oneness.

The psychiatrist Scott Peck makes the pregnant comment, "If we are going to use [community] meaningfully, we must restrict it to a group of individuals who have learned to communicate honestly with each other" (*The Different Drum*, p. 59). Christ's relationship with his Father underscores this idea. "The ground of [Christ's] communication with God was His communion with the Father" (Ray Anderson, *The Gospel According to Judas*, p. 48). *Communion* and *communicate* both come from the same root as *community*. Community requires honest and caring communication. Loneliness is not the absence of people but the absence of community. It is possible to be in a group of people without any sense of community.

The Goal of Forgiveness

Not to have a shared oneness with another person or persons is to be lonely indeed.

"The experience of being called the Beloved is the experience of communion. Communion is the word that responds to the deepest yearnings of the human heart. We are created for communion. I don't believe it is an exaggeration to say that what all people share is a lifelong search for communion." (Henri J.M. Nouwen, "Forgiveness: The Name of Love in a Wounded World," *Weavings*, Vol. VII, Number 2, March/April, 1992, p. 10).

My two older brothers were very close to each other and seemed able to communicate with each other almost without words. The two brothers just younger than I also seemed to pair off. While I enjoyed playing with my brothers and sisters, I was also very comfortable being alone with a book. Or I would sometimes go off on my bike and ride on back roads and trails (we lived away from the city). My relationship with my father tended to push me further into aloneness. If he did not believe I could do anything well, perhaps others felt the same way too.

The marvelous weekend conference I attended when I was nineteen began to move me more to communion, to fellowship. The sense that I was of real worth because Christ lived in me and the beginning of a new relationship with a person who became a close friend (and subsequently my wife), combined to begin drawing me out of myself and into new friendships with others, that is, into an alive community.

Two especially helpful passages of Scripture in this regard emphasize the richness and breadth of community. The first is John 17:20-23, which speaks of Christ's desire for community. This passage does not come from our Lord's teaching. It is, rather, the cry of His heart expressed in His moving prayer the night before His crucifixion. He prays for a oneness, a community, among His followers which is like the oneness He shares with His Father. He is not praying for a structure, for an organization, but for a relationship. *"The glory which thou hast given me I have given to them, that they may be one even as we are one"* (verse 22, RSV). The glory God has given Christ, Christ has given us with a view to oneness. What an incredible statement!

We do not often enjoy the level of oneness Christ expresses, a quality of oneness like that between Father and Son. An important aspect of the reason for this problem is that we confuse relationship and behavior. Volf has a superb treatment of Jesus' parable of the prodigal son (*Exclusion and Embrace*, pp. 156-165). The older brother could only think in terms of rigid obedience to rules. Relationship depended on whether the rules were followed or not. The father, however, "rejected this alternative because his behavior was governed by the one fundamental 'rule': relationship has priority over all rules. Before any rule can apply, he *is* a father to his sons and his sons *are* brothers to one another" (p. 164, emphasis his). Or again, a few lines farther on: "Relationship is prior to moral rules; moral performance may *do something* to the relationship, but the relationship *is not grounded* in moral performance. Hence the *will* to embrace is independent of the quality of behavior, though at the same time 'repentance,' 'confession,' and the 'consequences' of one's actions all have their own proper place" (emphasis his).

Two aspects of relationship and forgiveness need to be noted here. One cannot talk about forgiveness without realizing that there must be some degree of personal relationship with the wrongdoer.

For instance, drive-by shootings are common enough in our cities today. If the assailant and the victim are unknown to me, I may properly be angry at the wrong, but forgiveness is not the relevant response. The issues then are rather ones of justice and safety on the streets — matters about which I should be very much concerned. If the victim is my child or grandchild, that fact relates me

to the guilty one or ones, and the question of forgiveness enters into the equation. I cannot forgive
a person for the evil he or she does to others. I may
properly be angry for the evil a person does to others, and I am responsible for what I do with my
anger.

That anger can become a significant impetus to
work with others to bring about change in the
world. That response is good, but the "category" of
the action is not a subheading of forgiveness. We
do not forgive an act; we forgive the person who
does or promotes the wrong act. Forgiveness is a
relational transaction, and there needs to be some
personal relationship with the person if forgiveness
is to occur.

There is a second important dimension of relationship. The fact of a marriage relationship doesn't
say anything about the quality of the relationship.
Two married couples are equal in the fact of the
relationship. They may be worlds apart in the quality of their respective relationships. When I speak
about the importance of restoring a fractured relationship, I mean the quality of the relationship.
Forgiveness in the fullest sense wants nothing less
than a very warm and close fellowship between the
parties.

Our relationship with God is sometimes similar
to that of many marriages — a couple is still mar-

The Goal of Forgiveness

ried, but one or both partners is more concerned about self or other interests than he or she is about a healthy and vital relationship with the partner. That becomes a joyless marriage. So the goal of forgiveness is not merely a relationship that is quite empty, but rather one that is alive and joyful and richly satisfying to both parties, at least to whatever degree is possible in the particular situation.

Our understanding of our responsibility with reference to community must come to terms with our Model. God's desire in forgiving us is that we become part of His family in a close and joyful fellowship. We need to respond to Him, or His goal is not accomplished. Still, that quality of closeness remains His desire. God's desire is the pattern for us to follow in our relationships with others.

The goal remains, a goal Christ desires, a goal we want to move toward in our relationships. Relationships must be nurtured, cultivated, cared for. Christ also indicates that this quality of oneness has a purpose beyond its own intrinsic value, namely, *"that the world may believe that you have sent me"* (verse 21 — compare this with verse 23). The power of genuine oneness, of community, is very persuasive.

The second passage is Ephesians 2:11-19. Here Paul portrays the oneness that Christ makes possible among Christians. He does so by referring to the hostility that existed between Jew and Gentile, a virulent hostility present on both sides. But in Christ a tremendous change has taken place. He *"has destroyed the barrier, the dividing wall of hostility."* The former hostility is *"put to death."* Christ *"himself is our peace, who has made the two one."* The Gentiles *"are no longer foreigners and aliens, but fellow citizens with God's people"* (verses 14-19). Paul is saying that community is first of all between God and the forgiven person, but it does not stop there. It extends also to others in His family.

Phillips' paraphrase of verses 16-17 brings out the larger picture with startling clarity. Christ's death *"made utterly irrelevant the antagonism between [Jew and Gentile]. Then he came and told both you who were far from God and us who were near that the war was over."* Paul declares that Christ rendered the deep antagonism between Jews and Gentiles who have become Christians *"utterly irrelevant."* He announced *"that the war was over."* The same truth applies to other antagonisms and conflicts between or among Christians.

The *"utterly irrelevant"* is not easy to apply. When I was teaching in a black college in the South, my wife, two children and I lived in the black community where the college was located. An observation by my students surfaced several times: How can whites be Christians when they do not respect us as persons? It is a good question in the light of what Christ prays. My response admitted the problem, and I went on to point out that we all have blind spots. Part of the process of growing in Christ is to let His healing touch transform our blind spots.

From that situation in the South we moved to Beirut, Lebanon, where I taught in another college. There the animosity between Arabs and Israelis was at least as bitter as that between blacks and whites in our country. At that college, a large proportion of our textbooks were ordered from the United States. On one occasion, for a course on the life of Christ, I ordered a supplementary text. Of course the word *Israel* was used a number of times with reference to the time of Christ. To Arabs, the ancient use of the name was confused with the name of the modern state of Israel. I was directed by a senior official at the school to black out every occurrence of the word Israel in all copies of the text. Of course the students knew what was blacked out, but the school was protected by that device. That level of hostility runs deep indeed.

The antagonism of the Israelis against the Arabs was equally extreme. Whether with blacks and whites or with Arabs and Israelis, the bitterness often seemed as strong among Christians as among those who were not believers.

I mention one other example at a different level.

Restoring Relationships

In one church I served as an interim pastor I undertook to call on former members of the church who still lived within easy reach of the church, though they no longer attended. One of the people I saw was a woman who had been very active in the church some years before. After we visited a bit, I asked if there was any particular problem that had prompted her withdrawal. There was. Here is what she told me:

She often helped in the kitchen after any function where food had been served. On one occasion she was washing a few dishes and another woman was drying them. At one point the woman drying the dishes put a cup back in the wash because it wasn't completely clean. The woman I was visiting, who had been doing the washing, took offense at that and never returned to the church. What a tragedy! Although I suspect that this incident was "the straw that broke the camel's back," this woman obviously did not understand that *"the war was over,"* that her antagonism was *"utterly irrelevant."* "The gift of forgiveness will always feel incomplete if it does not bear fruit in reconciliation. ... Reconciliation means full restoration of a whole relationship" (Marjorie J. Thompson, "Moving Toward Forgiveness," *Weavings*, Vol. VII, No. 2, March/April 1992, p. 21).

When we experience God's forgiveness, when we become a part of His Body, the Church, the truth

The Goal of Forgiveness

of Ephesians 2:16-17 becomes actual. Paul liked the analogy of *"the body"* (see, for example, Romans 12, 1 Corinthians 12 and Ephesians 4). The various parts of a healthy physical body are a community, a oneness. The incredible complexity of the physical body is hardly noticed when all the parts are working together as a community. When they are not working together, we are ill. "The Pauline move is not from the particularity of the body to the universality of the spirit, but from separated bodies to the community of interrelated bodies — the one body in the Spirit with many discrete members" (Volf, *Exclusion and Embrace*, p. 48).

It often takes some time before the practice of the reality of the truth of our oneness in Christ becomes a part of our daily lives. The critical thing is that the basis for good relationships is in place. For a good relationship to become operational in our lives, we need, first, to recognize the truth of what God has done. We see it best in our new relationship with God. We are now part of His family. It also applies to our relationships within His family with other Christians.

Second, we need to enter into the process, not only to be willing but to align ourselves with what Scripture has said is true, namely, that the war is over, that the old antagonisms are *"utterly irrelevant."* Sometimes we need help from others with greater maturity in Christ to get new insights into dealing with a particular relational problem. We also need to be responsive to the Holy Spirit. I like the thrust of Jones' comment, "Christian forgiveness is not simply a word of acquittal; nor is it something that merely refers backward. Rather, Christian forgiveness — and, more specifically, for-given-ness — is a way of life, a fidelity to a relationship of friendship, that must be learned and relearned on our journey toward holiness" (*Embodying Forgiveness*, p. 66).

Third, since "wars" involve others, we need to initiate some peace moves; we need to talk with the other party or parties. That conversation needs to be undertaken gently, with the recognition that the problem may be primarily on our side.

Sometimes the other person may not even be aware of what we see as a problem. Those situations require very gentle handling. Boyer (*Finding God at Home*, p. 173) suggests that community primarily does two things: It provides a caring context, and it assists the caring persons to enlarge their scope.

The awareness of the truth of Ephesians 2:16-17 has profound implications for relationships within the Christian community. For example, in a marriage problem between a Christian husband and a Christian wife, the fact that the war has ended does

The Goal of Forgiveness

not do away with differences; it *can,* however, do away with the differences moving into resentment, antagonism, bitterness. Some years ago, my wife and I were part of the advisory team of a college Christian fellowship group at the college where I was teaching. One Sunday evening the program involved a panel talking about the areas of courtship and marriage. One of the panelists said she and her husband began their life together with the solid resolve that whatever problems might develop, divorce was not an option they would consider. Rather, they would work through problems as they arose.

We can have that same resolve in the Christian family, so that whatever problems or dissensions might develop with another Christian, resentment, antagonism and their like are simply not available choices. Negative responses don't just happen — we choose how we respond. This approach, whether in marriage or in other relationships, is not possible if one chooses to pursue his or her "rights," desires, etc., without regard for the other. In a community, we must deal thoughtfully and gently with others in the community, though recognizing that sometimes "tough love" is required. Differences are good and add variety and richness, as we see in nature. There is not simply one shade of green in the foliage of trees. Nor is there only one kind of tree or flower. We appreciate such variety in nature. People, too, are different from one another!

If we let differences move into resentment and bitterness, those qualities easily become hurtful and destructive. The problem, again, is not that we have differences. Differences bring richness to a relationship. As Archibald Hart says, we must seek for understanding, not necessarily for agreement (*Feeling Free*, p. 88). When I officiate at a wedding, just after the pronouncement of marriage, I emphasize by tone of voice our Lord's statement, *"Those whom God has joined together let no one separate"* (Matthew 19:6, my rendering). The "joining together" is not the end of differences! A "joining together" also happens as we become part of Christ's Body. Here, too, that does not mean the differences are at an end. Our oneness with other Christians needs to be cultivated and enjoyed.

In the community, we help one another in that process. Jones speaks several times of "forgiveness as a craft" (*Embodying Forgiveness*, pp. 218 and others). That also suggests the truth that forgiveness is an ongoing learning process. Because we cannot avoid wounding one another, we have many opportunities to keep learning the "craft"!

The example we have in Paul's letter to his friend Philemon who lived in Colossae is powerful. Onesimus, a slave of Philemon, had run away and

The Goal of Forgiveness

made his way to Rome. Runaway slaves found the inner city of Rome a good place in which to get lost. Somehow Onesimus came in touch with Paul, a prisoner in Rome at the time. Growing out of that, Onesimus became a Christian. Now Paul and Onesimus are brothers in Christ (in Colossians 4.9 Paul refers to Onesimus as his *"faithful and beloved brother,"* my rendering). So also are Onesimus and Philemon. Do Onesimus and Philemon know that the war is ended, that the former antagonism is now *"utterly irrelevant"*? As Paul and Onesimus talk, presumably over a period of some days, the decision is made for Onesimus to return to Philemon in Colossae. Did Onesimus suggest it, or did Paul? We don't know. That decision would have required significant courage on the part of Onesimus. According to the customs of the day, Philemon could have had Onesimus executed out-of-hand.

Paul writes a letter to Philemon and sends it with Onesimus. In the letter, Paul says, *"Perhaps this is the reason he was separated from you for a while, so that you might have him back forever, no longer as a slave, ... but ... a beloved brother."* Then Paul encourages, *"Welcome him as you would welcome me!"* (verses 15-17, NRS). That request is totally revolutionary in terms of the social mores of the day. A runaway slave and his owner beloved brothers in Christ? The war is over; the old antagonisms are *"utterly irrelevant."* If this is true for the deep hostility that had existed between Jew and Gentile, if it is true for the antagonism that existed between Philemon and Onesimus, it can be our experience also! That is what genuine forgiveness can accomplish when a spirit of forgiveness meets repentance. That is the goal of forgiveness! That is community.

In her *Learning to Forgive,* Doris Donnelly makes the profound comment, "To reconcile means to bring together that which belongs together but which is apart" (p. 70). That statement underscores the fact that forgiveness (Donnelly uses *reconcile* and *forgive* essentially as synonyms) must move toward togetherness, toward community. Forgiveness is not solitary; it is communal.

Salvation means becoming a part of the Body of Christ, where all the parts belong together. Hurting one another, offending one another, leads to separation, to tearing asunder "that which belongs together." It was the togetherness of the Christian community that led the ancient pagan to cry out regarding the Christians, "Behold how they love one another!" A spirit of forgiveness when wounding occurs, met with the expression of repentance, brings healing, brings forgiveness, brings reconciliation, brings wholeness, brings restored oneness. Jones' comment is worth repeating: "Christian forgiveness ... is a way of life" (*Embodying Forgiveness*, p. 66).

The Goal of Forgiveness

Again, the pattern God established in giving His Son portrays the reality. Our sin separates us from God; Christ died in order to make possible the family of God and our ongoing fellowship within the family; God's spirit of forgiveness meets our confession of our sin (repentance), resulting in our forgiveness. The "transaction" calls for celebration: " *'This son of mine was dead and is alive again; he was lost and is found!' And they began to celebrate"* (Luke 15:24, NRS). The celebration is both fitting and necessary. When we are hurt or when we hurt another, we need to reach out to express a spirit of forgiveness or our repentance, to seek to restore the troubled relationship. Doing something to celebrate renewed fellowship where there was alienation is good in itself. Might it also tend to discourage subsequent alienation between the two parties?

On beyond the specific hurts we do to one another, there is another layer of wrong. So often between fellow believers there is a kind of distance. We don't like or respond to another's appearance, lifestyle, understanding of the faith — or whatever. It isn't so much that we offend each other, but we fail to reach out, to seek to understand, to get to know, to learn from the other. In a word, while we belong together as a part of God's family, we don't endeavor "to bring together that which belongs together." Consequently, our individual lives, as well as our community, as well as our impact on the non-Christian world are all crippled to some degree.

It is worth pausing for a moment to consider the principal obstacle to community, indeed, to forgiveness. I think the central problem is self-centeredness. Self-centeredness turns our focus inward and excludes others, except as they may meet our needs. If my life strongly hinges on my desires, my hopes, my satisfactions, etc., it becomes very difficult to express either a spirit of forgiveness or repentance. (There is, of course, a proper concern about oneself — health, work, family, etc. I am not speaking here of that very legitimate concern.)

Self-centeredness manifests itself in many ways. Sometimes it is pride. Or it may be the flip side of pride, a lack of self-worth. Other times it is expressed in greed and unthankfulness. An absence of genuine caring is another expression. Can we not almost define sin as self-centeredness in opposition to God-centeredness? Self-centeredness is always destructive of relationships, sometimes very quickly, other times more gradually. One of the reasons my relationship with my father was a problem for so long was because I thought of forgiveness as a one-way street, from him (the wrongdoer!) to me. Not so. Forgiveness is always a two-way street.

The Goal of Forgiveness

How do we deal with the obstacle of self-centeredness? There is a radical way, a way that will expand to touch all facets of our persons, a way that opens onto some breathtaking vistas. Here we are at the heart and the glory of the Gospel, the good news of Christ. The language of the New Testament is striking. To let Christ into one's life is a new birth (see John 3:3) or a new creation (see 2 Corinthians 5:17). Neither figure means that all of our past history is removed, that we are somehow separated from all that has gone into making us what we are. On the other hand, we must not discount the newness, the freshness, the openness that is present in Christ. What makes the great difference, what is really new, is the fact that Christ comes into our lives (see Galatians 2:20).

The words seem so prosaic, but there is nothing prosaic about the fact. To be indwelt by deity, to have God's Holy Spirit enter our lives, is a radical change. I no longer struggle to change simply by my own effort. The resources of Almighty God are now available to bring about growing change. Part of the freshness and excitement of walking with Christ is the newness that is present in that kind of life. Walking in fellowship with the King of kings and Lord of lords can hardly be called boring!

Too often we prefer to remain restricted by the limits we put on ourselves. Our horizons become so circumscribed when we exclude God from our reckoning. The human person is an amazing being, even with all the problems we have from ignoring God. When we open ourselves to the One who designed us to walk in fellowship with Himself, then the possibilities are simply incalculable!

How do we begin to turn it all around so we become members of God's family, of our natural families, of friendship "families," of employment "families," who genuinely care for one another? The answer, in a word, is forgiveness. That is what this book is about, an attempt to clarify the richness of forgiveness and to move us toward a spirit of forgiveness and genuine repentance, toward community with God and with one another.

The sadness and loneliness of the absence of community was vividly demonstrated to me on one occasion. In a college where I was teaching, it was the practice to assign new freshmen each fall to various faculty members for help in advising regarding courses, and for whatever other help we could provide the new students. One fall, one of the students assigned to me was a bit unusual, though not in a way I could put my finger on. We met together two or three times and worked out his schedule to his satisfaction.

The first day of classes, I was in my study shortly before 8:00 A.M. This young man came to my door,

The Goal of Forgiveness

said he had ten minutes before class, could he talk with me. I invited him in and turned from my desk to face him. He didn't seem to have anything special on his mind. We chatted until he had to leave for class.

At noon that day I had a call from the president of the college asking me to come to his office. I went there, and a sheriff was with the president. They told me a young man from the college had driven three miles north of the college, turned off on a section road, had taken his clothes off and doused himself with gas. Then he had struck a match. Would I go with the sheriff to identify the body of the man who had stopped for a chat that morning?

As I thought about the young man, I wondered what kind of experiences, what sort of life, his had been. What had he gone through that left such hopelessness that he took his own life? I also wondered if I had been more alert, might I have picked up from our conversation that morning a cry for help? I don't know. I did not accuse myself of being responsible for his death, but might I have helped him if I had been more sensitive?

The sadness of the experience to me centered on the loneliness the young man must have felt. There were other students around, of course, but he apparently felt alone, without community. Rather than reaching out (unless his visit with me that morning had been such an attempt), he simply decided to end his life and, as suicide usually is, all alone.

Paul is speaking, in Ephesians 2, of the relationship between Christian and Christian. Likewise, Christ's prayer in John 17 is for members of his "family." In the case of relationships between non-Christians, or between a Christian and a non-Christian, the situation is somewhat different. It is certainly true that a spirit of forgiveness and repentance are essential for resolving relational problems, whether or not the parties are Christian, but there is not the further component of oneness in Christ. There is the oneness of shared humanity, which is in itself significant. With Christians, however, the forgiveness we know and experience in Christ brings about a oneness that provides a new base for the healing of relationships. While we Christians often don't do as well as we could in personal relationships, we have a foundation in Christ which non-Christians do not have.

I do not mean to suggest that Christians don't have significant differences! We do indeed have such differences. But in God's family, we have an actual relationship with one another. To use the family analogy that is so much a part of the New Testament, we are brothers and sisters in Christ. Forgiveness practiced among us keeps that family

The Goal of Forgiveness

closeness alive and healthy and warm. We not only share a common goal, a feature found in all sorts of groups and organizations, but we share a common life. We are part not merely of an organization but of an organism. Forgiveness is important not only because it maintains a closeness with God, but also because it maintains the warmth and closeness in our Christian family, within which we can wrestle with our differences.

We need to keep growing both in our understanding of the truths of Christianity, including our community, our oneness, and in the application of those truths to daily life. Growth is an essential element in the concept of life. Life is dynamic, not static. We never reach the place in our Christian life where there is not room for more growth — again both in understanding and in practice.

Of course, in many areas there will be a necessary opposition between Christians and non-Christians, for example, regarding the centrality of Christ for daily life or as the basis for ethics, etc. That opposition does not need to be marked by antagonism and bitterness, but the opposition in fundamental orientation is very real.

The new life in Christ has many facets which work toward the building of community. Here are a few of them: It is a life of faith working through love (see Galatians 5:6); it is a life under the control of the Holy Spirit (see Romans 8:5-6); it is a life of liberty (see 2 Corinthians 3:17 and Galatians 5.1); it is a life of joy (see Philippians 1:18 and 4:4); it is a life of thanksgiving (see Ephesians 5:20); it is a life which increasingly manifests the fruit of the Spirit (see Galatians 5:22-23 and others). As these realities become apparent in our lives, our community, our oneness, grows and is enriched.

These things are not suddenly and completely attained, but are a result of growth. The term *"fruit"* in Galatians 5:22 is expressive. Fruit is not the result of studied effort; it is not put on from the outside like the decorations on a Christmas tree. It is the product of life, the life of the Spirit of Christ. A healthy apple tree cannot *not* bear apples; it is the nature of the tree to bear apples. In the same way, a person who is growing in Christ cannot *not* bear fruit of the Spirit. As the child of God sees more and more of the light of the knowledge of the glory of God in the face of Christ, he is gradually changed into His likeness, from one degree of glory to another (see 2 Corinthians 4:6 and 3:18). (There is a quite marvelous illustration of this principle in the experience of Ernest in Nathaniel Hawthorne's lovely short story "The Great Stone Face.")

The foundation for this process of growth is beautifully stated in John 1:16: *"From his fullness we all received, even grace in place of grace"* (my render-

The Goal of Forgiveness

ing). The imagery of the Greek preposition *anti,* "in place of," is that of standing by a river. As the water immediately in front of one moves on, there is not an empty space. Rather, water takes the place of water — water in place of water. So in the Christian life there is always grace taking the place of grace, taking the place of grace, without end.

As Annie Johnson Flint wrote in the hymn "He Giveth More Grace":

His love has no limit, His grace has no measure,
His power has no boundary known unto men;
For out of His infinite riches in Jesus,
He giveth, and giveth, and giveth again!
— Annie Johnson Flint

Questions for Discussion

1. If forgiveness and community are as closely linked as I contend, why do you think Christians are as divided as we seem to be? What can we do as individuals to help fellow Christians realize that antagonisms between us are *"utterly irrelevant"*?

2. What are ways in which we can help the practice of the reality of our oneness in Christ develop?

3. Try imagining yourself as Philemon when Onesimus hands you Paul's letter. What do you think your response would actually be? Is that what you wish your response had been?

4. Consider Doris Donnelly's statement, "To reconcile means to bring together that which belongs together but which is apart" (p. 76). Discuss with a few others what the implications of that statement are.

5. What can we do to *"grow in the grace and knowledge of our Lord and Savior Jesus Christ"*?

Chapter 4

JUSTICE AND FORGIVENESS

A world of perfect justice is a world of love.
Miroslav Volf, *Exclusion and Embrace*

IN THE WHOLE MATTER of forgiveness, one of the most vexing problems is the relation between love (which we readily identify with forgiveness) and justice. We need to heed Hosea's great cry, *"Hold fast to love and justice"* (Hosea 12:6, RSV). We applaud Hosea's plea when love and justice work for our benefit. That is, we want to be loved, we want forgiveness. We also want to love (to extend forgiveness), but with a qualification: we want to love (forgive) whomever and whenever we wish. Caring for or forgiving anyone who has hurt us often holds little appeal for us. Similarly with justice, we very much want justice when we have been wronged. We are much less keen on justice when we are the wrongdoer.

We usually think of love (or forgiveness) and justice as being in an adversarial relationship: if you forgive, justice is ruled out; if justice is rendered, there can be no forgiveness. However, we do recognize that it is precisely because we love our children that we insist on discipline for wrongdoing, that is, on justice. Christians understand, at least dimly, that love (forgiveness) and justice are not in an adversarial relationship with God. The cross stands as a profound witness to God's love and justice. It is our Lord who takes away the sin of the world by taking the penalty of our sins (justice) on Himself. He does so out of love.

Charles Williams has a striking statement: "Sin is the name of a certain relationship between man and God. When it is fixed, if it is, into a final statement, he gives it other names; he calls it hell and damnation. But if man were to be restored, what was to happen to the sin? He had a name for that relationship too; ... he called this 'forgiveness' " (*The Forgiveness of Sins*, p. 33).

Our response to gross wrong commonly follows a different pattern from God's response. For instance, a young woman is seized, carried off, raped and murdered. The parents of the girl are

Justice and Forgiveness

devastated and deeply angry — rightfully so. If anyone suggests forgiveness, the parents' response (whether Christians or not) will often be some variation of: "Forgive? You must be crazy. I hope the man is caught and rots in jail!"

In reality, justice and forgiveness are not incompatible. If the culprit in my example is caught, he should receive a severe penalty, not because of vengeance, but because a society must safeguard its citizens, must have penalties appropriate to the crimes. While forgiveness would be very difficult in such a situation, it does not stand in contradiction to justice. The structures of society require appropriate sanctions for wrongdoing, that is, justice; broken relationships require forgiveness.

The connection between justice and forgiveness is not easy to grasp. There are abundant biblical witnesses to the justice of God, a justice that is essential because of His total holiness. At the same time, there are also overwhelming biblical witnesses to God's love, to His concern to bring about right relationships with Himself and with people. At the cross, these two dimensions meet with radical sharpness and power. To refuse God's offer of forgiveness via the cross is to refuse salvation.

Sin must be judged, not because some rule says so, but because of the character of God. There are two options: the death of Christ for us if we choose to accept God's provision, or ultimate separation from God in the final judgment. In the first, justice is rendered by Christ's death on the cross; in the second, the person experiences God's justice directly in the final judgment.

Our responsibility as Christians is to share the good news of what God has done for us, and to demonstrate the good news of what He continues to do in us. The concern is not for "my rights" (compare Philippians 2:8-11), but for how we can help each other grow. Our lives as well as our words are to witness to God's incalculable love. That witness becomes increasingly effective as we keep growing in the grace and knowledge of our Lord and Savior, Jesus Christ (see 2 Peter 3:18). The wrongdoer does not have a right to forgiveness. Justice demands appropriate punishment, but love rules out a demand for forgiveness.

Forgiveness, by God or by people, is always from grace. Augsburger expresses this concept very effectively: "The basis for reaffirming perceptions of love for another who is seen as a wrongdoer is the profound awareness that I-you-we are of infinite worth, in spite of, apart from, with no dependence on appearance, performance, effectiveness or any other external criteria" (*Caring Enough to Forgive* ..., p. 38). So Christ died for us "in spite of, apart from, with no dependence on appearance, performance, effectiveness or any other external criteria." We are loved!

We are back again to following the Model God has given us. Like God, we are to love, to reach out to the wrongdoer while hating the wrong. At one college where I taught, there was a retired professor of psychology who could not accept the distinction that it was possible to love the wrongdoer but hate the wrong. He believed the person could not be separated from the person's acts. C.S. Lewis, in *Mere Christianity*, comments that he previously had the same problem my retired friend had. Then he realized he regularly made the distinction with himself: "However much I might dislike my own cowardice or conceit or greed, I went on loving myself. There had never been the slightest difficulty about it. In fact the very reason why I hated the things was that I loved the man" (Book III, chapter 7).

We need to learn to do with others what we do with ourselves. Unlearning an old, well-established habit is difficult. Again, we have our Model to help us. God hates the evil we do while continuing to love us and to help us move in a new direction as long as we live. Where would we be otherwise?

At times, because we live in a very imperfect world, it may be the case that our only choice is between evils. Then we have to choose the lesser of the evils. We confess the problem to God and go on from there. The Christian is never called on (biblically) to say that wrong is right. We must recognize that the determination of wrong is sometimes very difficult, and Christians will not always agree whether particular acts are wrong. The Christian way of life is not a commitment to finding and judging evil. It is, rather, a commitment to walk in love. *"The entire law is summed up in a single command: 'Love your neighbor as yourself' "* (Galatians 5:14). Augsburger has a powerful statement: "Wrongdoing is not a valid reason for my refusing to value and love another" (... *to Not Forgive,* p. 60).

We need to distinguish between our living in society and our personal relationships with people of the society. In society, we need a judicial system to safeguard the well-being of the community. Wrongdoers in the society must be judged and appropriate sanctions applied (not every wrongdoer should go to jail!). What the society does is different from what we do in personal relationships.

I like Gregory Jones' *Embodying Forgiveness* very much, but I think he does not adequately clarify the difference between society's sanctions and personal relationships. He raises the question, for instance, "Are there not some people whom it is better to hate and to desire vengeance against, particularly in the absence of repentance? ... Or, put

Justice and Forgiveness

more in social and political terms, isn't 'retributive punishment' appropriate as a society's way of expressing its revulsion against particular offenses? If not, how are such themes as punishment and accountability related to forgiveness ... ?" (p. 242). "Retributive punishment" is appropriate for a society; forgiveness is not the task of a society. A society is authorized to administer punishment (for example, see Romans 13:1-7). Forgiveness depends on the attitudes of the wronged person and of the wrongdoer.

In personal relationships, punishment is not the primary concern. Often, punishment is not a fitting concern at all. The primary concern in broken relationships is the possibility of restoring the closeness of the relationship. That restoration requires repentance on the part of the wrongdoer and a spirit of forgiveness on the part of the wronged person. Administering punishment to the wrongdoer does not exclude a spirit of forgiveness on the part of the wronged person.

It is society, not the wronged person, that must administer justice. Whether the relationship is healed or not, in no case am I authorized to become, in Carnell's fine phrase, a self-appointed "administrator of justice" (*Christian Commitment*, pp. 103 and others) or to hate the wrongdoer. It is appropriate to hate the wrong. God

Restoring Relationships

is our Model. He hates the wrongs we do, but continues to love us and seeks to restore the broken relationship. For us, it is much easier to make that statement than it is to practice the truth of the statement!

The case of children is a bit different. Parents have the responsibility of teaching their children what is right and of disciplining them appropriately when they do wrong (justice). In the home, children are to learn love and justice and the nature of forgiveness, a "lesson" that is not the primary responsibility of society at large.

The punishment assessed by society pays the claims of justice at the societal level when our legal system is at its best. Part of the ongoing anger of a victim and his or her family is because the system is often not at its best. However, the incompleteness of human justice does not render forgiveness impossible. Justice will always be rendered either by Christ's death on the cross or by the guilty person's ultimate punishment on the other side of death.

While justice is an aspect of God's nature, judgment is not the thing God delights in. Isaiah speaks eloquently: *"The Lord will rise up ... to do his work, his strange work, and perform his task, his alien task"* (Isaiah 28:21). His "strange," or "alien," work is judgment. Judgment is not God's first choice. While He must judge because evil is incompatible

94

with His holiness, it does not bring Him joy. We can see a parallel with parents of young children. It is sometimes necessary to discipline children. It is not the thing that gives parents pleasure, but it is necessary in the whole process of the child's development.

In 1 John 4:7-16, we have the statement twice repeated that *"God is love."* In the same passage, the same context, John tells us that God gave His Son *"to be the atoning sacrifice for our sins"* (NRS). The atoning sacrifice (justice) springs from love. The New Testament tells us that our forgiveness by God is only because justice has been rendered. Christ took the penalty for our sins at the cross. God so structured the universe that sin must come under judgment. His character is such that He cannot disregard sin.

Christ's death on the cross is a once-and-for-all event that makes possible God's forgiveness of us. "Over our heads and without our consent something has been done by God in Christ by which our status has been changed from slavery to sonship" (H. F. Lovell Cocks, *By Faith Alone*, p. 139). There is no counterpart to that act in our experience. That is to say, we do not have to undergo some similar experience to Christ's before we can forgive another for wronging us.

Is the reason for that fact part of the grandeur of

what Christ did for us? Catch your breath! Can we not say, must we not say, that His death not only paid the penalty required by God's justice, but that it also paid the penalty required by our justice when we have been wronged? We don't get what we deserve; Christ got what we deserved at the cross. That is grace! When we express the spirit of forgiveness toward one who has wronged us, that attitude is possible because the "sentence" for that wrongdoing has already been served. So we, too, are free to express grace!

If Christ pays, not only the cost of our forgiveness by God, but also the cost of our forgiveness of others, justice is not set aside; it is provided by another. Because we are not responsible for its administration, we are free to work on the relationship, and we can be generous in spirit with the wrongdoer. Sometimes truth is hard to grasp, but that does not weaken its quality as truth! And sometimes the truth is even more difficult to explain. In this area we are fumbling with profound but also glorious mystery! Authentic forgiveness really is possible!

Our society holds up impartiality as the standard for justice. In many situations, that is appropriate. For instance, it is intolerable for an official in a sports contest to make calls that favor one side in the game. That mistakes are sometimes made by such officials is recognized, but the official cannot deliberately make decisions that help one contestant or one team. Our treatment of minorities in our country doesn't suggest a very deep commitment to impartiality!

Miroslav Volf, in his profound book *Exclusion and Embrace*, takes us farther: "The knowledge of justice depends on the will to embrace. ... Embrace is part and parcel of the very *definition* of justice" (p. 220, his emphasis). He sharpens the issue even more: "There is a profound 'injustice' about the God of the biblical tradition. It is called *grace*" (p. 221, his emphasis). Or again, "If you want justice without injustice, you must want love. A world of perfect justice is a world of love" (p. 223).

Any human society has to have some kind of judicial system. That is, each society has to have some consequences for wrongs that are destructive to the society. Because we are prone to take advantage of one another, every society establishes standards for its citizens. The particular forms and penalties vary from society to society. Such judicial systems are prima facie evidence of the reality of sin among people everywhere. In the administration of justice there is no room for vindictiveness. Revenge is not the same as justice. Revenge is a retreat to *"an eye for an eye"* in a personal sense with, of course, some interest! There is no objectivity in revenge — only the desire to make the other person suffer.

In addition, all human beings become involved in relationships — family, friendship, business, sports, etc. It is impossible to establish laws to govern all aspects of relationships. That is one reason why love is so crucial. *"For the whole law is fulfilled in one word, 'You shall love your neighbor as yourself' "* (Galatians 5:14, RSV). If we act with one another in love, we will not deliberately hurt one another. And when we do hurt one another, love reaches out to restore the broken fellowship. Relationships are always at risk; the hurts we do to one another can fracture and destroy those relationships.

Our Lord makes our responsibility with others very specific: *"If [another] sins against you* [in this case you are the innocent party], *go and tell him his fault* [you take the initiative], *between you and him alone"* (Matthew 18:15, RSV). Similarly, if you are the wrongdoer, notice Christ's words also: *"So if you are offering your gift at the altar, and there remember that [another] has something against you* [the other person believes you wronged him/her], *leave your gift there before the altar and go; first be reconciled to [the other], and then come and offer your gift"* (Matthew 5:23-24, RSV). These two passages show what is implicit in love, namely, that love requires a reaching out to the other whether you are the wronged person or the wrongdoer. Love, in God or people, is not satisfied with separation nor with a truce.

In personal relationships, the question is not whether a person has a right to forgiveness but rather whether any person can be demeaned or treated wrongly. Christianity answers the latter question with an emphatic NO. The holiness of God cannot condone any wrong, whether action, attitude, word or thought, that we do to another. The glory of the Christian message is that God Himself in Jesus Christ has graciously taken the penalty for our wrongbeing and our wrongdoing. *"For our sake [God] made [Christ] to be sin who knew no sin, so that in him we might become the righteousness of God"* (2 Corinthians 5:21, RSV).

The biblical understanding of the nature of human beings is that we bear the image of God. Because love and justice are part of God's person, they are also part of our being. People do not have to be Christians to love. The capability of love is a part of our nature as humans. Indeed, neither God nor we are free *not* to love. The normal human being cannot *not* love, though we are altogether too selective in our application of love!

This inherent ability and motivation to love struggles with self-centeredness. Without Christ, the self-centeredness more often wins. So the common attitude in a conflict is, "If you will be good (or fair, or ...) to me, I will be so to you." But we almost invariably start with the other person, "If you ..." We rarely say, "Whatever your attitude toward me, I care for you and want our relationship to be healthy." When we become Christians, we have a new dynamic, the presence of the Holy Spirit. As we are responsive to Him, love begins to win in the struggle with self-centeredness. The struggle does not end: We begin to understand, at least faintly, that the dignity of the person, the other as well as myself, demands the expression of love.

Similarly, neither God nor we are free to set aside justice. The normal human being cannot escape a sense of indignation when the dignity of his or her person is not respected. Of course, the degree of indignation varies with the degree of affront. We want justice when we are wronged, but not when we do the wrong! We are sensitive to wrongs to our own person, but are much less sensitive to the wrongs which we do to others! When we are wronged, we often quietly shift from forgiveness of the one who hurt us to fairness. "It is only fair" that the person who wronged me should somehow pay or suffer for that wrong. However, we don't want fairness from God; from Him we want grace!

When my family moved to the South where, as I

Justice and Forgiveness

said before, I taught for some years in a black college, we quickly became aware of the huge differences between attitudes toward blacks and whites. How can one justify separate drinking fountains for whites and "coloreds"? Or separate rest rooms for white women and white men, but only one rest room for "coloreds," both men and women? Or the Christian white woman who had a black lady who worked for her three or four days a week. At lunch time, the white would fix lunch for the black, but the black could not eat off the white person's ordinary china. Instead, the white woman had some dime-store heavy white china for the black. But on a regular basis, the black lady saw the white put her own plate on the floor for her dog to lick. The black lady could not eat off the regular dishes, but the dog could lick the plate! Neither love nor justice can defend such practices.

It is little wonder that the blacks finally rose up in rebellion at a system that condoned such treatment. And we all saw the television news pictures of nonviolent marchers met with dogs and water cannons. The black rebellion brought about significant legal changes with regard to the races; attitudinal changes take place much more slowly! American Indians, Hispanics and Asians have had all too similar experiences in our country.

As Christians, we begin to realize, dimly at first,

that justice is a two-way street, not only for us, but also for others. Again, the dignity of the person, both myself and the other, demands justice. Rather than seeing love and justice in an adversarial relation, it is these two facets of our inherent being as humans which stand at the foundation of all society. God is sensitive to the wrongs against Him, the wrongs against all human beings everywhere and the wrongs against His world. Seeing God as our Model has far-reaching implications!

I spent the 1960s and 1970s as a college professor. Students at the time were generally very restive with college rules and desired more freedom. Yet, if someone "ripped off" a particular student's sound system, the cry was for justice, for application of the rules! That is not uncommon. We demand justice for wrongs done to us, but we are rather quiet about justice when we do the wrong. Indeed, when we do the wrong, we attempt to "justify" our action! When we are wronged, we often seek to "get even," and that response speaks to our deep concern for justice. Both love and justice demand that the dignity of the person be respected, whether our dignity or that of others.

Our problem is that we see love and justice through the prism of our own self-centeredness. Thus, we focus on the benefits of love and justice for ourselves. We slip over the "otherness" of love and justice because we miss the fact that both love and justice are essentially other-directed. The result is growing self-centeredness and a loss of closeness in our relationships. When love is dominant in a relationship, wrongs that occur are more easily reconciled because of the openness to each other and the caring that exists. It is also true that love makes us more vulnerable to hurt!

God expresses justice as well as love and calls for us to show justice as well as love. Both the quality of God's justice and the demand for us to be just is portrayed over and over in the prophets. What we see often in Scripture is that love and justice work together. As an example, *"to loose the chains of injustice"* (Isaiah 58:6) is not only a requirement of justice but also one of love. Self-centeredness works against both love and justice. God longs to be the center of our being; in other words, we need to be God-centered.

We live in a world with an excess of bitterness and hate and injustice. God's people urgently need to hold fast to love and justice. To do so requires the exercise of forgiveness. Once again, forgiveness does not mean the setting aside of justice. It does mean we are not free to become resentful and bitter, or to become our own "administrator of justice."

Christ's death on the cross provides a crucial contrast. On the one hand, in the hatred of the religious leaders and in the expediency of Rome, love and justice wither and die. On the other hand, the cross is the supreme monument to God's love and justice. God's love and justice do not wither or die! Because of Christ, Christians "can stand in [God's] presence without any sense of guilt, condemnation, or inferiority" (Kenyon, *In His Presence*, pp. 216 and others). What a wonder!

Questions for Discussion

1. In situations where you have been wronged, how did you handle the forgiveness/justice relationship?

2. Do you find my differentiation between the "structures of society" and "broken relationships" (p. 89) helpful?

3. I have stated that Christ's death "not only paid the penalty required by God's justice, but that it also paid the penalty required by our justice when we have been wronged" (p. 96). Does that observation open some new possibilities regarding forgiveness in your thinking?

4. How do you react to the quotation from Kenyon that Christians "can stand in [God's] presence without any sense of guilt, condemnation, or inferiority" (p. 104)?

Chapter 5

CONTINUING THE QUEST

But keep growing in the grace and knowledge of our Lord and Savior Jesus Christ.
2 Peter 3:18, my rendering

FINALLY, IT IS NECESSARY TO raise a two-pronged question: How do we learn and teach forgiveness? Both parts of the question apply to our natural children and to our "spiritual" children.

The key to the answer is example. We are not going to make much progress "doing" forgiveness until we have experienced forgiveness. To experience genuine forgiveness requires an open and receptive heart. The greatest possible experience of forgiveness is to receive God's forgiveness. Here again, the thrust of Jesus' powerful story in

Restoring Relationships

Matthew 18 is eloquent. The man who experienced the king's forgiveness (the "hundred and fifty thousand years" variety) was judged severely because, having experienced that level of forgiveness, he closed his heart to his peer who owed him a sum that was paltry by comparison (the "three and a third month" variety).

The teaching of forgiveness, particularly in the home with young children, is not best accomplished by "lecture." It is better accomplished by the child's seeing forgiveness in the day-to-day life of his or her parents, and by having the parent express repentance to the child when the parent wrongs the child. Wronging one's children inevitably happens. Thus the child has the opportunity to show a spirit of forgiveness — he or she is not always the one in the wrong! In the context of love, a spirit of forgiveness and repentance are rather readily learned.

Still, the process can become quite complex. If a parent is not self-accepting, it will be very difficult for that parent to express genuine repentance. In addition, if the parent is not self-accepting, it will be very difficult for the child to grow up with genuine self-worth. Rather, the child will more likely be self-rejecting. A low level of genuine self-worth makes forgiveness a very difficult process. For a Christian, a great way to build self-worth is to understand that we are *"accepted in the beloved"* (Ephesians 1:6, KJV), that Christ lives in us (see Galatians 2:20), that God accepts us as we are with all of our shortcomings and failures.

We don't have to try to clean up our lives before we are accepted by God. He helps us in that process after we become His children through faith in Jesus Christ. He doesn't leave us where we were; the Holy Spirit begins the lifelong process of conforming us more and more to Christ. The expression "God is not done with me yet" is on the mark. Hence we need to be gentle and patient with one another as we teach one another and learn from each other.

As new creations in Christ, the Holy Spirit helps us to *"grow in the grace and knowledge of our Lord and Savior Jesus Christ"* (2 Peter 3:18). To grasp the marvelous fact that we are truly accepted by God, who knows fully our hearts, minds and actions, is to give us a new sense of who we are. Thus, we experience a growing level of self-worth. Children can understand God's acceptance very naturally if their parents are positive and affirming towards them. That parental acceptance does not mean ignoring the wrong things children do. Indeed, ignoring wrong behavior is destructive to self-worth because it conveys the idea that the parents don't care. Children need parameters set by the parents, but those guidelines must be established and enforced in a context of love and acceptance of the person of the child.

God sets parameters for all of us. The fact that He graciously does so does not mean that we can slide over them. Here again, God is the Model for parents. To love children does not mean permitting them to "do their own thing" or to do "what comes naturally." It rather means to affirm children in positive ways and to help them understand what it means to be courteous and thoughtful with people and to walk responsibly with God.

As children grow toward maturity, parents need to give them greater freedom to make decisions appropriate to their level of development and to hold them responsible for their decisions. That process is difficult both for parents (who want to keep control too long) and for children (who want greater freedom too soon). Where there is active love, the difficulties can be negotiated, though often with some struggle on both sides.

Learning forgiveness is best accomplished by seeing it modeled in the home. Teaching forgiveness is most effective when the parents can demonstrate to children their own practice of forgiveness with each other and with their children. That context is the best environment for learning.

Continuing the Quest

My experience with my father speaks to the radical need for teaching our children by example and by word, both a spirit of forgiveness and repentance. If our children never hear us, their parents, express a spirit of forgiveness and repentance, should we be surprised that it does not come easily to them? We need to learn how to break out of our "fear-full" defensiveness. Surely one of the ways to do that is to become aware of the amazing depth of God's forgiveness of us, the forgiveness that is of the "hundred and fifty thousand year" variety.

When forgiveness is not learned in the process of growing up, it is much more difficult to learn as an adult. But it is not impossible! To experience God's forgiveness is a huge first step. Jesus' story in Matthew 18 is again relevant. It is also very helpful to have a friend who has walked some distance along the road of a spirit of forgiveness and repentance share his or her experiences with troubled relationships. Even without such a friend, articles and books on forgiveness as well as classes and discussion can also help us in our quest. At some point, however, we simply have to "bite the bullet," as the common expression puts it. We must choose to cultivate a spirit of forgiveness when we are wronged, and we must choose to express our repentance when we are the wrongdoer. Each of us is responsible to reach out to bring healing to relationships. C.S. Lewis offers us some practical advice:

> *When you start mathematics you do not begin with the calculus; you begin with simple addition. In the same way, if we really want (but all depends on really wanting) to learn how to forgive, perhaps we had better start with something easier than the Gestapo* [Lewis was writing in the context of World War II]. *One might start with forgiving one's husband or wife, or parents or children ... for something they have done or said in the last week .*
> (*Mere Christianity*, Book III, chapter 7)

It is encouraging to remember that with the issues and process of forgiveness we never reach the point where there is not more to learn!

In summary, here are the crucial points:

1. Our primary model for the practice of forgiveness is God Himself. We are to forgive others *"just as in Christ God forgave [us]"* (Ephesians 4:32).

2. In order to experience forgiveness, there needs

to be a true spirit of forgiveness on the part of the wronged person. That means openness to the wrongdoer, care for and reaching out to the one who did the wrong. Equally necessary is a sincere repentance on the part of the wrongdoer, a genuine sorrow for having hurt the other person or persons. The matter can become very complex because often when we have been wronged, we have hurt the other person as well. *Humility* and *gentleness* are the operative words in working through broken relationships.

3. The purpose of forgiveness is to bring about community, first with God, and second with others. Some degree of community is possible with non-Christians, but it does not reach the depth nor the comprehensiveness possible in union with Christ. In that oneness with Christ, antagonisms between and among Christians are made *"utterly irrelevant."*

4. The alternatives to forgiveness are consistently negative and destructive to wholesome relationships. Forgiveness is positive and constructive.

5. It is essential for us to recognize that forgiveness and justice are not adversaries. These two

realities are not in an either/or relationship. In personal relationships, we should concentrate on demonstrating a spirit of forgiveness and on repentance.

When all is said and done, there are elements that simply cannot be reduced to any formula. We cannot understand all of the dimensions involved in God's grace. The guidelines we are given in Scripture we seek to follow. As our sensitivity grows, our practice of forgiveness also grows. Always, we must remind ourselves that we cannot box God in to our continually limited awareness of His grace. Humility is an appropriate attribute in our explanation of God's Word! We need to keep growing *"in the grace and knowledge of our Lord and Savior Jesus Christ"* (2 Peter 3:18). Part of the wonder and joy of the Christian life is that we can keep progressing in both our understanding and our practice of living with and for Jesus Christ.

Three statements from Scripture provide the best conclusion:

"God so loved the world that he gave his one and only Son, that whoever believes in him shall not perish but have eternal life."
John 3:16

Continuing the Quest

Be kind and compassionate to one another, forgiving each other, just as in Christ God forgave you. Ephesians 4:32

And we all, with unveiled face, beholding the glory of the Lord, are being changed into his likeness from one degree of glory to another; for this comes from the Lord who is the Spirit.

2 Corinthians 3:18, RSV

Questions for Discussion

1. Did your parents enrich your growing-up years by practicing forgiveness in their relationship with each other and by helping you learn forgiveness?

2. If you are a parent or one who has a position of responsibility with young children, how do you think the children would evaluate your example regarding forgiveness?

BIBLIOGRAPHY

Anderson, Ray. *The Gospel According to Judas* (Colorado Springs: Helmers Howard Publisher, 1991).

Arvin, Newton, ed. "The Great Stone Face," *Hawthorne's Short Stories* (New York: Vintage Books, 1946).

Augsburger, David. *Caring Enough to Forgive/Caring Enough to Not Forgive* (Ventura, California: Regal Books, 1981).

Augustine. *Confessions* (New York: Penguin Classics, 1961).

Boyer, Ernest, Jr. *Finding God at Home* (San Francisco: Harper, 1998).

Bultmann, Rudolph. "Aphiemi," *Theological Dictionary of the New Testament*, Vol. I, edited by Kittel, Gerhard & Friedrich, translated by Geoffrey Bromiley (Grand Rapids: Wm. B. Eerdmans Publishing Co., 1964).

Calvin, John. *Institutes of the Christian Religion* (The Library of Christian Classics), edited by John T. McNeill, translated by Ford Lewis Battles (Philadelphia: The Westminster Press, 1960).

Carnell, Edward John, *Christian Commitment* (New York: The Macmillan Company, 1957).

Cocks, H.F. Lovell. *By Faith Alone,* in Library of Contemporary Theology (London: James Clarke & Co., Ltd., 1943).

Restoring Relationships

Donnelly, Doris. *Learning to Forgive* (Nashville: Abingdon Press, 1979).

Hart, Archibald. *Feeling Free* (Old Tappan, New Jersey: Fleming H. Revell, 1979).

Jones, L. Gregory. *Embodying Forgiveness: A Theological Analysis* (Grand Rapids, Wm. B. Eerdmans Publishing Co., 1995).

Kenyon, E.W. *In His Presence,* (Lynnwood, Washington: Kenyon's Gospel Publishing Society, 1994.

Koeberle, Adolf. *The Quest for Holiness,* translated by John C. Mattes (Minneapolis: Augsburg Publishing House, 1936).

Lewis, C.S. *Mere Christianity* (New York: The Macmillan Company, 1958).

Lewis, C.S. *The Problem of Pain* (London: Fontana Books, 1957).

Murphy, Jeffrie G., and Hampton, Jean. *Forgiveness and Mercy,* (Cambridge Studies in Philosophy and Law) (New York: Cambridge University Press, 1988).

Nouwen, Henri, J.M. "Forgiveness: The Name of Love in a Wounded World," *in Weavings* (Vol. VII, Number 2, March/April, 1992).

Owen, John. *The Glory of Christ* (Wycliffe Series of Christian Classics) edited by Wilbur M. Smith, (Chicago: Moody Press, 1949).

Palmer, Earl. *1, 2, 3 John & Revelation* (The Communicator's Commentary) edited by Lloyd J. Ogilvie (Dallas: Word, Inc., 1982).

Peck, M. Scott. *The Different Drum* (New York: Simon & Schuster, 1988).

Bibliography

Rhode, Melody Goddard. *Forgiveness, Power, and Empathy* (unpublished doctoral dissertation in clinical psychology; facsimile by U.M.I., 1990).

Schechter, S. *Some Aspects of Rabbinic Theology* (New York: The Macmillan Company, 1910).

Smedes, Lewis. *Forgive and Forget* (New York: Pocket Books, 1984).

Thompson, Marjorie J. "Moving Toward Forgiveness," *Weavings* (Vol. VII, Number 2, March/April, 1992).

Volf, Miroslav. *Exclusion and Embrace* (Nashville: Abingdon Press, 1996).

Williams, Charles. *The Forgiveness of Sins* (Grand Rapids: Wm. B. Eerdmans Publishing Co., 1942).

Yancey, Philip. *What's So Amazing About Grace?* (Grand Rapids: Zondervan Publishing House, 1997).

To contact the author:

Ralph A. Gwinn
19334 King's Garden Drive, R-103
Shoreline, WA 98133
206-546-7973